SURVIVALIST SAM STOCKS UP

THE FOUR B's OF PREPPING FOR KIDS

Written by Kermit Jones, Jr.
Illustrated by Christy Brill

For Abby, the inspiration of Survivalist Sam!
– K.E.J.J.

Visit
www.PrepperPeteAndFriends.com
to learn more!

Join our community
www.facebook.com/PrepperPeteAndFriends

Text copyright ©2014 by Kermit E. Jones, Jr.
Illustrations copyright ©2014 by Christy Brill
Cover design and digital layout by Jeff Eskridge
All rights reserved. Published by Kamel Press, LLC.

Library of Congress Control Number: 2014917541

No part of this book may be reproduced, stored in a retrieval system, or transmitted by any means, electronic, mechanical, photocopying, recording, or otherwise without written permission from the author.

978-1-62487-037-8 Paperback
978-1-62487- 038-5 Hardcover
978-1-62487- 039-2 eBook

Published in the USA

There once was a squirrel
named Survivalist Sam.

A Survivalist is someone
who stocks up supplies
and learns skills for the future.

As a squirrel, Sam is used to stocking up whenever he can. He and his friend, Prepper Pete have been planning together for a long time.

It's good to have friends!

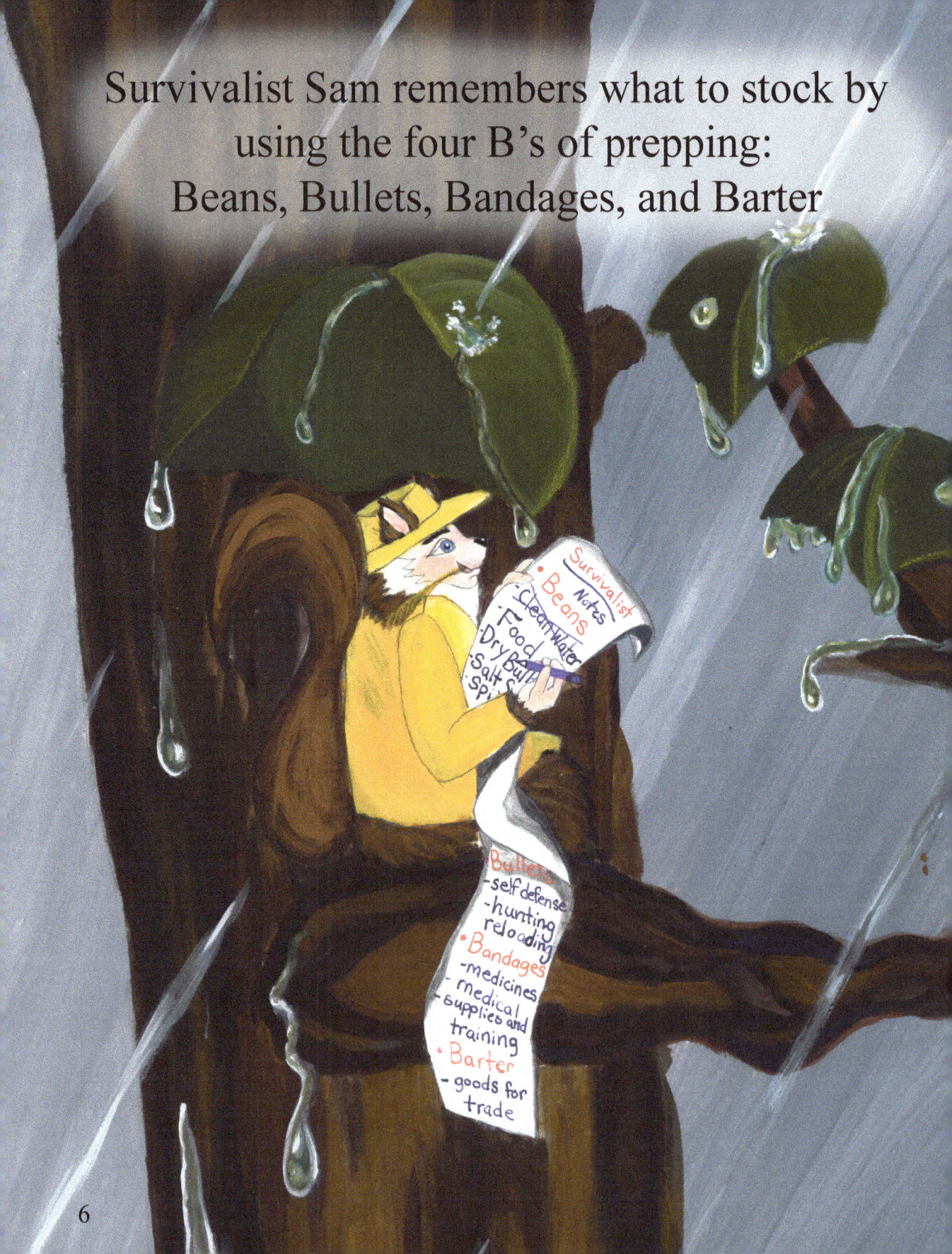

Survivalist Sam remembers what to stock by using the four B's of prepping: Beans, Bullets, Bandages, and Barter

"Beans" reminds us that it's very important to have plenty of clean water to drink and food to eat.

Beans, rice, and grains are usually the biggest part of a food storage plan. When stored properly, they can last a very long time.

Salt, sugar, and spices are important, too.

Salt preserves food; sugar and spices make it taste yummy!

Sam learned to plant and grow a garden using completely natural seeds, often called "non-hybrid" or "heirloom" seeds.

Non-hybrid vegetables allow him to harvest his own seeds so he can grow more vegetables the next year.

Many Survivalists and Preppers "can" their extra vegetables.

Canning is a special way of storing food for a very long time.

They make sure they have food and supplies to take care of their pets for a long time, too!

After Beans, "Bullets" reminds Survivalist Sam about protection. This includes shelter, as well as guns and ammunition, which can be used for hunting and defense.

The Constitution makes sure people can legally own guns, also called firearms.

The 2nd Amendment says we have a "right to bear arms."

Hunting is an important skill that allows Sam to feed his family.

He is careful to not waste anything. He uses the skin to make clothing and other parts to make tools.

Sam knows there might be people who haven't prepared, and they may try to take the things they need.

Some of them are bad guys, but some are just desperate or scared.

Survivalist Sam wants to be able to hunt and defend his family and friends for a long time.

He has supplies and tools for reloading.

"Reloading" means he can make his own ammunition in the future.

When Beans and Bullets are taken care of, Sam thinks of Bandages.

"Bandages" reminds him of things he doesn't need every day, but are still important. This includes things like medical supplies and educational books.

Survivalist Sam and Prepper Pete have taken classes on first-aid.

This is so they can help people in need both now... and in the future.

Sam knew he didn't have supplies or training for every topic, so he built a survival library.

Books can teach people lots of ways to survive and those skills can be taught to others.

When stores are empty, people might want to trade for all sorts of things.

The last "B" stands for "Barter" which means "to trade things" instead of simply paying with money.

Many things will become valuable, such as a good knife, books…

…and even toilet paper!

Survivalist Sam knows he can also use his barter supplies for charity. He wants to help people whenever he can.

So when your family stocks up, even if it's just for storms, hurricanes, tornadoes, or floods, remember the four B's of prepping...

- Beans
- Bullets
- Bandages
- Barter

Sam agrees with Prepper Pete. "Some people prepare because they are afraid.

Our family doesn't have to be afraid… because we are prepared!"

So stock up,

sleep well,

...and keep prepping!

A NOTE FOR GROWNUPS

The topic of stocking up doesn't have to be reserved for prepping and survival! Many activities, from gardening and canning, to first aid and reading, can engage kids of all ages to learn useful skills that will prepare them for the rest of their life.

The Four B's are important in many situations, though sometimes in a different order. Talk to your kids about safe shelter in a storm, or being aware of strangers; take a first aid class with them to learn new skills. Encourage reading and critical thinking.

Don't scare… prepare!

KEEP PREPPING!

So stock up,

sleep well,

…and keep prepping!

A NOTE FOR GROWNUPS

The topic of stocking up doesn't have to be reserved for prepping and survival! Many activities, from gardening and canning, to first aid and reading, can engage kids of all ages to learn useful skills that will prepare them for the rest of their life.

The Four B's are important in many situations, though sometimes in a different order. Talk to your kids about safe shelter in a storm, or being aware of strangers; take a first aid class with them to learn new skills. Encourage reading and critical thinking.

Don't scare… prepare!

KEEP PREPPING!

LOOK FOR THESE OTHER BOOKS ABOUT PREPPER PETE & FRIENDS!

PREPPER PETE PREPARES
There are many reasons to prepare! Join our favorite Prepper as he introduces kids to some of them!

PREPPER PETE'S GUN OF A SON
When he turns old enough, Pete decides to take his son to a gun safety course where they learn important safety rules to follow.

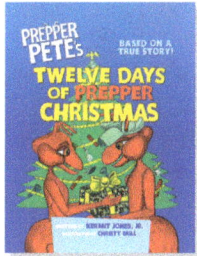

PREPPER PETE'S TWELVE DAYS OF PREPPER CHRISTMAS
Twelve perfect gifts for the Prepper in your life! Based on a true story.

PREPPER PETE'S BE PREPARED!
Is your family ready? Join our favorite Prepper as he helps kids understand what they can do to be better prepared for emergencies they might face! Parents can verify that their children know what to do!

PREPPER PETE GETS OUT OF DODGE
When the time comes to leave town, our hero grabs his family and takes them to safety using OPSEC (Operational Security) along the way.

Visit www.PrepperPeteAndFriends.com for more!

ABOUT THE AUTHOR

Kermit Jones, Jr. stumbled across the idea of a prepper book for kids when trying to decide how to explain the topic to his four young daughters. Having grown up in a rural setting, he went on to graduate from the U.S. Naval Academy and serve for over a decade on Active Duty, first as a Surface Warfare Officer and later as a Navy Chaplain. Between his kids and his career, he has learned that it's important to always "be prepared!"

ABOUT THE ILLUSTRATOR

Christy Alexander Brill is a native of Wilmington, NC. Proudly married to a United States Marine, and the mother of three young children, she understands the importance of being prepared.

JOIN OUR COMMUNITY!

- FREE BOOK DRAWING EACH MONTH!

- SIGN UP FOR OUR NEWSLETTER TO GET TIPS FOR WORKING WITH CHILDREN AND NOTIFICATION OF NEW RELEASES.

PREPPING IS ALWAYS MORE FUN WITH FRIENDS!

PrepperPeteandFriends.com

www.ingramcontent.com/pod-product-compliance
Lightning Source LLC
Chambersburg PA
CBHW041436040426
42453CB00019B/2447